Inside the World's Most Infamous Terrorist Organizations

The ETA
Spain's Basque Terrorists

Wayne Anderson

The Rosen Publishing Group, Inc.
New York

In loving memory of Gerald E. Gladney, that wonderful soulmate who encouraged me to give up numbers for words, and to Joshua George Anderson, who insisted that I study my letters

Published in 2003 by The Rosen Publishing Group, Inc.
29 East 21st Street, New York, NY 10010

Library of Congress Cataloging-in-Publication Data

Anderson, Wayne.
The ETA : Spain's Basque terrorists / Wayne Anderson.— 1st ed.
    p. cm. — (Inside the world's most infamous terrorist organizations)
Summary: Discusses the origins, philosophy, and most notorious attacks of the Basque separatist group ETA, including their present activities, possible plans, and counter-terrorism efforts directed against them.
Includes bibliographical references and index.
ISBN 0-8239-3818-2 (library binding)
1. ETA (Organization)—History—Juvenile literature. 2. Terrorism—Spain—Paâis Vasco—History—20th century—Juvenile literature. 3. Nationalism—Spain—Paâis Vasco—History—20th century—Juvenile literature. 4. Paâis Vasco (Spain)—Politics and government—20th century—Juvenile literature. 5. Paâis Vasco (Spain)—History—Autonomy and independence movements—Juvenile literature. [1. ETA (Organization) 2. Terrorism—Spain—Paâis Vasco. 3. Nationalism—Spain—Paâis Vasco. 4. Paâis Vasco (Spain)—History—Autonomy and independence movements.] I. Title. II. Series.
HV6433.S72 E8518 2003
946'.6082—dc21
                                                                    2002007768

Manufactured in the United States of America

Contents

Introduction

Basques are an ancient people who were among the earliest settlers of an area that today straddles the border between Spain and France. They are ethnically distinct from the Spanish and French, possess an entirely different language, and are steeped in separate cultural traditions. Much of their history has been characterized by desperate attempts to preserve this unique culture and their independence from waves of violent invaders.

In 1959, a group of young Basque activists founded Euskadi ta Askatasuna (ETA), which translates as "Basque Homeland and Liberty," a group devoted to an armed struggle to win independence for the Basque region of Spain from the latest "invader"—Spain's fascist dictator, General Francisco Franco. Since then, the ETA has killed more than 800 people and has wounded thousands of others in its quest for an independent homeland.

From the outset, the government of Spain has treated the ETA as a terrorist organization. At times, the Spanish government has taken extreme police measures in its efforts to eliminate the ETA. The organization has also been the target of several violent right-wing groups who oppose the idea of a breakup of Spain. Over the years, thousands of ETA members and supporters have been killed, tortured, or imprisoned by the Spanish government.

Despite a number of halfhearted peace negotiations between the ETA and the Spanish government, and in spite of several splits

Spanish police investigate the scene of an ETA car bombing that killed five people and injured twelve others in Madrid on December 11, 1995. The ETA commits violent acts in an attempt to force the Spanish government to pay attention to its political demands.

within the ETA over the continued relevancy of the struggle, the Basque insurgency continues. Still, the organization has not come close to achieving its goal. Why, in the face of such lack of progress, does the ETA soldier on? The Basques consider themselves distinct from the Spanish, a separate nation. They treasure what they regard as their right to govern themselves. The ETA is a die-hard manifestation of this Basque nationalism.

The History of Basque Nationalism

CHAPTER

Basque Country (called Euskal Herria by the Basques) is situated in the borderland between northern Spain and southern France. The area under French administration is referred to as Northern Basque Country, or Iparraldea, and the area under Spanish control is known as Southern Basque Country, or Hegoaldea. In total, there are seven provinces in Basque Country. Four provinces are in Spain and have Spanish and Basque names: Navarra (or, in Basque, Nafaroa), Guipúzcoa (Gipuzkoa), Vizcaya (Bizkaia), and Alava (Araba). The three French provinces have French and Basque names: Labourd (or, in Basque, Lapurdi), Basse Navarre (Benafaroa), and Soule (Tuberoa). The entire area is only 8,218 square miles (roughly 20,600 kilometers), which is about the size of the state of New Jersey. The Spanish side of the border has 86 percent of the territory and 91 percent of the nearly 3 million people of Euskal Herria.

An Ancient People

The Basques have occupied this territory for at least several thousand years—over 40,000 by the estimation of some historians and archaeologists. The Celts, the Carthaginians (from present-day northern Africa), and the Romans encountered them there as early as the third century BC. The Basques fought to preserve their land, language, and culture against a succession of invaders, including

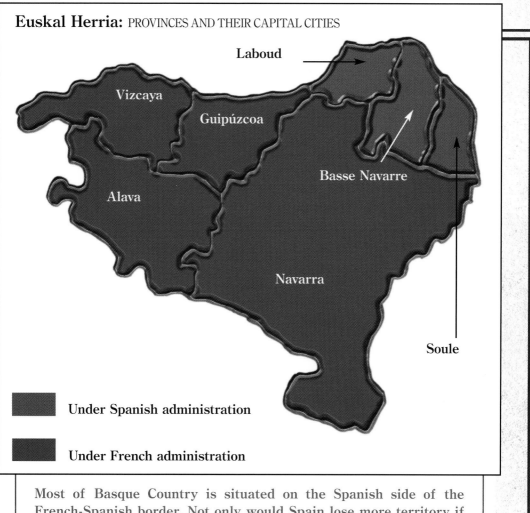

Euskal Herria: PROVINCES AND THEIR CAPITAL CITIES

Laboud

Vizcaya

Guipúzcoa

Basse Navarre

Alava

Navarra

Soule

■ Under Spanish administration

■ Under French administration

Most of Basque Country is situated on the Spanish side of the French-Spanish border. Not only would Spain lose more territory if an independent Basque state were to be created, it would also suffer a great blow to its economy since Spanish Basque Country is one of the country's most industrialized regions.

the Visigoths (a medieval Germanic people), the Moors (Arab conquerors of Spain), and the Franks (another medieval Germanic people who occupied parts of modern-day France and the Netherlands). Even more remarkable than their ability to hold on to their tiny patch of land in the face of this series of invasions is the Basques' success in preventing their culture from being erased

Tens of thousands of Basques watch as folk dancers hold torches during a 1998 celebration of the official Basque language, Euskera, in a soccer stadium in Bilbao, Vizcaya. No matter what their view of the ETA, traditional Basques are passionate nationalists who turn out in great numbers for events that promote Basque culture.

or absorbed by the surrounding tribes and nations that always seemed to be pressing against them.

Basques possess a unique language, Euskera. It is spoken only in this tiny region and is not related to any other known language in the world. Yet Euskera was spoken in western Europe long before the ancestors of all the other modern western

The Basque Kingdom

The kingdom of Navarra was the first and only Basque state that ever existed. Established in 818 AD under Inigo de Aritza, the kingdom evolved out of the need of the Basque people to move into fortified towns because of the constant warfare with invaders. Under the rule of Sancho III ("the Great") in the twelfth century, the kingdom included all seven provinces of the Basque region. Sancho the Great also captured Burgos and other territories from the kingdom of Castile, and he made Navarra the most powerful kingdom on the Iberian Peninsula (the land mass that includes modern-day Spain and Portugal). Under Sancho VII ("the Strong"), the kingdom began to disintegrate. The provinces of Vizcaya, Guipúzcoa, and Alava broke away after a bitter political dispute and became integrated with Castile by 1200.

When Sancho the Strong died in 1234, the ruling family had no more heirs, and the Navarrese turned to the French province of Champagne and submitted to its ruling family. In 1512, Spain's King Ferdinand invaded Navarra, pushing its French rulers and their army northward beyond the Pyrenees mountain range. It was then that the current border between Spain and France was established, permanently dividing Basque Country between the two nations. The Basque kingdom of Navarra lasted approximately 700 years.

European languages were introduced there. This fact leads many linguists to claim that Euskera is Europe's oldest living language and leads some historians to speculate that the Basques are the "original Europeans."

As Mark Kurlansky observes in his book *The Basque History of the World*: "It must have been an isolating experience, belonging to this ancient people whose culture had little in common with any of its neighbors. It was written over and over in the records of those who observed the Basques that they spoke a strange language that kept them apart from others. But it is also what kept them together as a people, uniting them to withstand Europe's great invasions."

Alliances of Convenience

Throughout the Middle Ages, the Basque region was a collection of self-governing provinces that boasted strong democratic traditions. Facing increasing attacks from larger nations, the Basque provinces were forced into alliances with the larger kingdoms of France and Castile (which would later join with the kingdom of Aragon to become Spain). Under these special relationships, the Basque provinces were gathered into the French and Spanish kingdoms, but they maintained their right to self-determination (the freedom of a group to choose its own political future). Eventually, however, Basque autonomy (self-government) became a victim of the mounting pressure in both France and Spain to create strong, centralized governments and unified nations.

The French Revolution began in 1789 and dealt a tremendous blow to Basque autonomy and set off a chain of violent struggles that pitted not only Basques against Spaniards, but also Basques against Basques. In France, the victorious revolutionaries abolished the special Basque rights, known as feuros, and fused the

This painting depicts the storming of the Bastille—a prison in Paris where political prisoners and enemies of the king were held and tortured. On July 14, 1789, a mob of French revolutionaries, with the help of some of the king's own troops, attacked and destroyed the Bastille and released its imprisoned inmates. This violent uprising marked the beginning of the French Revolution.

three Basque provinces with another region, Béarn, into a single département (similar to an American state). These moves, together with the current French policy to make all regions "equally French," have so far successfully muted claims for autonomy inside Northern Basque Country.

The reaction of the Spanish Basques to the dramatic changes taking place in France was surprising. For the most part, they were so excited about the democratic ideas of the Enlightenment, the overthrow of the monarchy, and the news of the establishment of parliamentary rule in an elected republic that they showed little concern for the plight of the Basques in France.

When the French revolutionaries crossed the border into Spain in 1793, they encountered little resistance from the Basques in the province of Guipúzcoa—some towns even welcomed them—and easily overwhelmed the Spanish troops who had moved in to stop them. Soon the French overran and occupied most of the Spanish Basque provinces and threatened the rest of Spain.

By their inaction against the French invaders, the Spanish Basques had breached the special relationship they had with Spain. Many in Madrid, led by the outraged military, began to question whether the Basques should enjoy special rights if they could not be counted on to defend the Spanish border. They also argued that Spain would be better off with a strong centralized government instead of the existing system that gave significant power to regional authorities.

The Liberals, as the forces for centralism were called, came to power in 1812. Since then, there has been a long and often bloody struggle between centralism and regionalism in Spain, with one of the central questions being what to do about the Basque provinces.

This is a scene of a street in the Spanish Basque town of Guernica after it was destroyed by German bombers in 1937. The attack was ordered by the fascist General Franco during the Spanish Civil War, a conflict that Germany, also a fascist nation at that time, joined and supported.

The Rise of Franco

It was against this background of conflict, in 1895, that Sabina Arana y Goiri, fearing the erosion of the Basque language and culture, founded the Basque National Party (Partido Nacionalista

Thousands of Basque youths raise their fists and flash peace signs before a copy of Pablo Picasso's famous 1937 painting "Guernica" during a demonstration on April 26, 1977, marking the fortieth anniversary of the bombing of the Basque town of Guernica, which the painting commemorates.

Vasco, or PNV) to be a political vehicle to press for reforms and greater autonomy. By the mid-1920s, the party developed deep roots within the Basque region, especially among the youth, and became a major voice for Basque concerns. Nevertheless, the PNV would not make any progress toward the goal of regional autonomy until 1936, when Spain's first democratic government declared the Basque region to be autonomous.

The History of Basque Nationalism

This victory was short-lived, however. A military coup attempt in 1936, led by General Francisco Franco, escalated into the Spanish Civil War, which lasted three years. The rebels won the war, and Franco became dictator of Spain in 1939. This was a disastrous result for the PNV and the Basques, who had supported the defeated democratic government during the civil war. The Basques, who had suffered terrible loss of life during the war against Franco's forces (including the 1937 bombing of the Basque town of Guernica by German aircraft under Franco's command), were now singled out by him for revenge. Not only did Franco ban the PNV and order the death, imprisonment, or torture of Basque leaders and soldiers who had not managed to flee into exile, but he also confiscated the properties of Basque nationalists and outlawed public displays of Basque identity, including the speaking of Euskera. He met any display of Basque nationalism with ferocious military action.

Instead of stamping out Basque culture and shattering the dream of Basque independence, however, Franco's oppression provoked even greater anti-Spanish feeling among the Basques, made them more aware of their ethnic heritage, and united them as a political force. Soon groups of Basques began meeting secretly to discuss what might be done. Some members of the exiled democratic government returned to Basque Country, and workers began organizing themselves into illegal labor unions. The time was ripe for a militant resistance to Franco's violent dictatorship. The ETA would soon step in and fill that role.

The Birth of
the ETA

Following Franco's brutal rise to power, all hope for Basque independence seemed to be dashed. Yet if Franco believed that violent repression would be enough to break the Basque spirit, he gravely underestimated his foes. With the formation of the ETA, he would quickly meet an adversary whose will was even greater than his own.

Out of Frustration, a Movement Is Born

The ETA had its origins in a small group of university students who began meeting in 1952 to discuss Basque politics, increase their awareness of the Basque nationalist movement, and promote the use of Euskera. From these discussions, the students began to publish an underground journal called *Ekin* (which in Basque means "to act"), a name by which the group would come to be known. They soon formed an alliance with the PNV's youth movement but quickly withdrew out of frustration with the PNV's passive resistance to Franco's oppression. Ekin believed that, as always, Basques would have to fight for Basque rights, not simply wait for them to be granted by the Spanish.

For a while, the PNV had been waiting for the United States and its World War II allies to overthrow Franco and restore democracy in Spain. In addition, the party's leaders claimed to

General Francisco Franco smiles as he reviews a military parade in 1939. Throughout his rule Franco used the military to suppress dissent, especially in the Basque region. As a result, members of the military were, and continue to be, preferred targets of the ETA.

have been assured by members of the ousted Spanish government that the autonomous status of the Basque region would automatically be restored if and when a democratic regime was reinstated. In exchange, the PNV promised not to seek further separation from Spain.

Ekin regarded this deal as unacceptable. To the group, anything short of complete independence—a separate nation—would be a betrayal of Basque interests. With its membership growing as a result of the defection of members of the PNV's youth movement and the recruitment of students at Deusto University in Vizcaya, Ekin became the ETA on July 31, 1959.

In a short time, the group began spray painting its initials on walls in larger Basque cities and burning Spanish flags, signaling its intention to be a major force in the future of Basque politics.

The ETA's Debut

The ETA's first challenge to the Spanish authorities was a highly symbolic attack upon General Franco's rule. On July 18, 1961, the group tried to derail a train carrying Franco supporters to a celebration in San Sebastian, Guipúzcoa, for the twenty-fifth anniversary of the military coup that began the Spanish Civil War. The ETA had been so careful not to cause any casualties that it failed to derail a single car. Nevertheless, more than 100 eterras, as ETA members became known, were imprisoned and another hundred forced into exile in Franco's retaliation for this assault.

The crackdown severely stalled the group's operations in Spain. Nevertheless, it gave the exiled leaders in France, who organized themselves into the Executive Committee, some time to think about the direction of the organization. In 1962, the Executive Committee released its first public statement, declaring that it was a secret organization intent on gaining Basque independence as soon as possible and through whatever means necessary, including violence. The Franco regime was officially put on notice of the ETA's intentions and seriousness.

A New Commitment to Violence

Despite its initial illegal political activities, the ETA did not commit many violent acts during much of its first decade of operation. For most of those years, its leaders were engaged in energetic debates over the philosophy and strategy of the organization. The debate, which took place at all levels of the ETA, was played out in discussion meetings, conventions, the organization's magazine, *Zutik*, and a number of other publications ranging from pamphlets to books.

The consensus that emerged in 1967 was that the ETA should pursue an ideology of armed struggle in support of not only Basque independence but also a socialist agenda that would empower the working class. Recognizing that direct confrontation with the Spanish government's security forces would be suicidal, however, the ETA developed a strategy known as the action-repression-action spiral theory.

According to this theory, the ETA would provoke the Spanish government into committing repressive acts in response to the ETA's carefully targeted terrorist attacks and its intervention in popular causes, such as union strikes. For every police reaction by the government, the ETA would commit an even more provocative act, encouraging the government to react with even greater force. The level of violence and repression would escalate to such an unbearable level that the population would eventually rise in rebellion against the government and, in the chaos of the ensuing civil war, the Basques would seize the opportunity to break away from Spain.

Youth Groups

Radical groups that embrace violence as a way to achieve their goals generally appeal primarily to the young. The ETA is no different, enjoying its greatest support among Basque youths. The organization has successfully inspired and mobilized a large section of young people, many of whom have organized themselves into ETA youth groups. These youth groups regularly organize protests and street violence, distribute threatening posters, and firebomb or sabotage symbols of the Spanish state.

In a *New York Times* report of March 8, 2002, on a Spanish police raid against Segi, a prominent ETA youth group, Spain's interior minister Mariano Rajoy is quoted as saying, "The initiation of youths into these type of activities provides a nursery which then feeds ETA command cells."

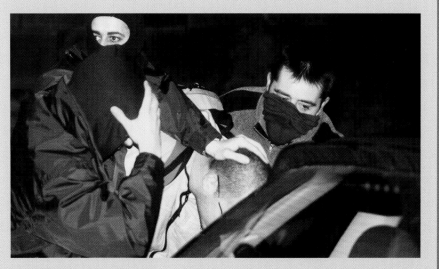

Masked police officers arrest an alleged member of the ETA-affiliated youth group Segi in Bilbao, Vizcaya, on March 8, 2002.

Theory in Action

The death of a popular eterra named Etxebarrieta at a police roadblock in 1968, and the resulting public outcry throughout the Basque region, provided the ETA with an opportunity to test the spiral theory. On Friday, August 2, of that year, the ETA assassinated Melitón Manzanas, who had acquired a reputation as a brutal police commissioner who enjoyed torturing Basque nationalists. It was the ETA's first planned execution.

As if on cue, Franco's response came swiftly and ferociously. The following Monday, he declared a state of exception (a suspension of constitutional rights) in the Basque region that lasted for months. Thousands of Basques, most of whom had nothing to do with the ETA, were arrested and tortured. Some were even convicted and sentenced to years in prison for "crimes against the state" that had nothing to do with Manzanas's execution.

With many of its members in jail, on the run, or in exile, and its network of cells disrupted, the ETA was ill equipped to step up its provocation of the Franco regime according to the spiral theory. What little resistance the group did offer to Franco's repression was met with the brutal might of the dictator's security forces.

A Failed Theory, a Groundswell of Support

Ordinary Basques, undaunted by this fierce crackdown, demonstrated and went on strike in support of the ETA within the Basque region, and a swell of student riots, unrelated to the Basque cause, swept across all of Spain. In January 1969, Franco extended the state of exception to cover the entire country in an attempt to put a lid on all organized dissent, especially in the Basque provinces.

By killing Manzanas, the ETA had sparked what seemed to have been an ideal test of the spiral theory. But despite Franco's repression, there was no larger rebellion, no nationwide civil war. Disappointed, a weakened ETA was forced to abandon the spiral theory after its first trial run. To many eterras, it seemed too costly a tactic, especially because the police counterterrorist measures had left the organization so broken that it could not effectively respond. The ETA simply could not control the pace of events or the ferocity of government response once the spiral was set in motion.

Eventually, sixteen ETA leaders were tried for killing Manzanas; one was acquitted, and the others received long prison sentences after having first been sentenced to die. The court-martial (a trial conducted by members of the military), held in the province of Burgos in December 1970, was widely regarded as unfair for both its procedures and its verdict. As a result, it was an international public relations disaster for Franco. Angry mobs marched on Spanish embassies in other Western European countries. Several countries issued statements condemning the trial while others ordered their ambassadors to return home from Spain (a major diplomatic slap in the face).

The ETA's reputation among the Basque people skyrocketed during the trial. Its members, particularly those who would be tried, were hailed as heroes to such an extent that even the PNV, long criticized by the ETA for being too passive, announced in one of its publications that it was no longer opposed to the use of violence in the struggle for self-governance. Ordinary workers went on strike during the trial, and, emboldened by this support, ETA members shouted nationalist slogans and sang nationalist songs in the courtroom.

Admiral Luis Carrero Blanco, General Franco's long-time supporter and trusted advisor, worked his way up from undersecretary in 1942 to prime minister in 1973. By the early 1970s, it was clear that he was the only person Franco trusted to rule Spain should the dictator become ill or die. Known to the ETA as "the Ogre," Carrero Blanco masterminded the crackdown on illegal labor unions and many counterterrorist campaigns against the ETA.

Near collapse only a year before, in 1970 the ETA began to see a marked upsurge in both its membership and its popularity as a result of its stand against Franco. And though its leaders—many of them new and inexperienced—were divided over strategy and the overall direction of the organization, the ETA would rally within a couple of years to carry out what is widely regarded as its boldest and most spectacular attack: the assassination of Spanish prime minister Admiral Luis Carrero Blanco.

Raising the Stakes

Carrero Blanco was Franco's most trusted adviser and the man whom many considered to be the aging dictator's most likely successor. The ETA, who called Carrero Blanco "the Ogre," saw him as the man who would continue Francoism after the aging Franco was dead. So, in 1972, when the ETA learned that Carrero Blanco had established a pattern of attending Catholic Mass regularly—with very little security—at the Jesuit Church of St. Francisco de Borja in Madrid, ETA leaders decided to kidnap him. By doing so, they hoped to secure the release of more than 150 imprisoned ETA members. Their plans eventually changed to assassination when they realized that it would be far easier to kill Carrero Blanco than it would be to kidnap him (which would require a complicated plan and split-second timing). More important, it was decided that killing him would have more significant political repercussions.

For months, ETA operatives in Madrid watched Carrero Blanco's movements to verify his routine. When they realized that his car stopped at the exact spot at about the same time every morning, they determined how they were going to kill him.

Posing as sculptors, ETA commandos rented a basement apartment near Carrero Blanco's church in late November 1973. By December 7, they began digging a tunnel under the street. Ten days later, when the tunnel was complete, they set up explosives below Carrero Blanco's parking spot. At 9:30 on the morning of

Emergency personnel scour the scene of the assassination of Spanish prime minister Luis Carrero Blanco on December 20, 1973. The assassination is widely believed to have been a major turning point in Spain's political history, resulting in the end of Franco's dictatorship and the beginning of a more democratic form of government.

December 20, the commandos, disguised as electricians working on cables on the street, set off 165 pounds of dynamite, hurling Carrero Blanco's car several stories in the air over the top of a church building. Carrero Blanco, his bodyguard, and his driver died instantly.

The coffin of General Francisco Franco is carried through the streets of Madrid during an elaborate funeral ceremony in November 1975. The general's death ended one of the most troubled periods in Basque and Spanish political history.

Striking a Blow Against Francoism

Historians disagree over the significance of the assassination of Carrero Blanco in the course of Spanish politics, but at the time it was widely seen as the end of Francoism. By this time, Franco, who was said to have become very depressed by the death of his intended successor, was visibly ill, and opposition leaders secretly began planning for a transition to democracy in anticipation of the dictator's death. Franco continued to order the arrest and persecution of ETA leaders—six were officially charged for killing Carrero Blanco. This time around, however, the ETA was better organized to deal with his reprisals.

Not everyone in the ETA approved of the Carrero Blanco assassination. This philosophical disagreement set off a series of struggles for control that would eventually result in a permanent split in the organization. In 1974, two groups emerged from the divided ETA: The ETA (politico-militar), or ETA (p-m), which favored a combined strategy of socialist politics and armed struggle, and the ETA (militar), or ETA (m), which preferred to operate as a small, secretive organization passionately committed to a single agenda: the armed struggle for independence.

Though splintered, the two groups stepped up their activities over the next year by killing members of Spanish security forces, bombing important buildings, kidnapping rich industrialists for ransom, and fanning the flames of public unrest. Franco responded with a stream of state-of-exception decrees in the Basque provinces that themselves led to greater unrest in the form of strikes, riots, and mass demonstrations. Clashes between the police and demonstrators became commonplace. The Basque region was in a state of chaos. Nothing Franco tried was successful in restoring order. He had lost control.

General Franco's last state of exception was still in force when he died on November 22, 1975. He had not solved Spain's perennial Basque problem. He had not destroyed the ETA.

The ETA in Democratic Spain

Franco's death cleared the way for a return to democracy in Spain. Within days, Spain's new ruler, King Juan Carlos I, declared an amnesty for nearly all of Spain's political prisoners. Operating as a figurehead, Juan Carlos would allow Spain to be governed by a freely elected parliament and prime minister. The Basques were cautiously hopeful that these developments would move them closer to self-determination.

The New Constitution and an Offer of Autonomy

Adolfo Suarez, who became prime minister in 1976, negotiated a deal with most of the previously illegal opposition that led, first, to the legalization of political parties; next, to the election of a parliament in June 1977; and, finally, to the ratification of a new constitution by popular vote in December 1978.

The new Spanish constitution included a provision for the creation of territorial units—known as autonomous communities—in recognition of the various ethnic nationalities that make up Spain. Despite being shut out of the drafting of the constitution, and in spite of the widespread boycotting of the vote to ratify the constitution in their provinces, Basque political leaders quickly began negotiations to gain autonomous status for Spanish Basque Country. In 1979, the Autonomous Basque Community of Euskadi

Juan Carlos de Borbón is installed as king of Spain during a proclamation ceremony on November 22, 1975, restoring the monarchy in Spain after nearly forty years of dictatorship. Francisco Franco's death had paved the way for Juan Carlos to become king and head of state.

was created. To the disappointment of many Basques, however, the province of Navarra declined to join the other three Spanish Basque provinces and would later become a separate, autonomous community.

Although the Basques did not get the full independence they had wanted, autonomous status guaranteed the Basques their own local governments and parliaments, school systems, highways, and police force, and gave them a degree of control over their own taxes. In addition, for the first time under Spanish rule, Euskera became co-official with Spanish as the language of the region. The Ikurinna, the long-outlawed Basque flag, became the official flag of the Autonomous Basque Community of Euskadi.

The Slow Pace of Change

Despite these gains, a significant number of Basques, and many in the ETA, were not satisfied. To these Basques, the autonomous region was a mockery of Basque nationalism and the quest for complete independence from Spain. Their displeasure was further aggravated by how slow and seemingly reluctant the central government in Madrid was to transfer real administrative power and needed resources to the new autonomous region. Moreover, street demonstrations and strikes in the Alava province in 1976 were strongly suppressed by riot police, leading to the deaths of five Basques and the injuries of countless others.

Many Basques concluded that there was little difference between the level of police brutality under Franco and under Spain's new democratic regime. It was the issue of amnesty, however, that would cause the greatest friction between the Spanish government and the Basques during the period of transition to democracy.

At the time of Franco's death, there were approximately 750 Basques in prison for political crimes. Despite the amnesty immediately declared by King Juan Carlos and vigorous negotiations between the regional Basque government and the central government, it would be another couple of years before most of these political prisoners would be released.

During this time, both factions of the ETA stepped up their activities to try to force the Spanish government to act more quickly. These activities included kidnappings, bombings, and assassinations of police officers, suspected informers, and even Basque mayors who were thought to have been Franco supporters. By the end of 1977, when all but ten of the original political prisoners had been released, the ETA had killed twenty-six people, wounded seven, and kidnapped three.

Frustrated by the impatience of Basque political leaders, continuing unrest among Basques in general, and, above all, the increasing violence of the ETA, the Spanish government in 1978 instituted tough new antiterrorist laws and police measures that included suspension of constitutional rights and suppression of some kinds of political expression. The ensuing crackdowns by the Spanish authorities led to the imprisonment of a new set of political criminals, which would in turn drive the ETA to further violence. For the next few years, the number of Basques in prison rose steadily, and the government of Spain came under increasing criticism from Amnesty International (a group committed to protecting the human rights of prisoners worldwide) for allegations of torture and other human rights abuses.

To Negotiate or Not to Negotiate?

Aside from fighting for independence and the release of political prisoners, both the ETA (p-m) and the ETA (m) tried to adapt to the newly democratic Spain—a country that now allowed the formation of political parties and organizations. Both groups joined a socialist organization called Koordinadora Abertzale

Sozialista (KAS, or the Socialist Patriotic Coordinator), which included political parties and labor unions whose aim was to work as a unified coalition representing the interests of the Basque working class.

In 1977, the ETA (p-m) formed a political party called Euskadiko Ezkerra (EE), or Basque Left, which won a seat in the Spanish parliament and another in the regional Basque parliament. By this time, there was a growing movement within the ETA (p-m) that favored a negotiated end to violence. The pro-negotiation faction reasoned that complete independence from Spain was an unattainable goal and that, with Spain becoming a democracy, it was possible to further Basque causes by generating popular support and working within the democratic system at both the regional and national levels.

Many ETA members strongly disagreed with this position, touching off a long power struggle within the ETA (p-m) that eventually led to the anti-negotiation faction quitting the organization for the more militant ETA (m). Left in total control of the organization, the pro-negotiation eterras began making overtures to the Spanish government, while not yet abandoning their violent tactics, which would continue for several more years.

The ETA (m) formed its own political party and considered joining in peace negotiations during Spain's transition years. Seeing the early success of Euskadiko Ezkerra, the ETA (m) formed Herri Batasuna (People's Unity) in 1978. In that same year, the ETA (m) announced its willingness to discuss a cease-fire if five conditions were met. This list of conditions included:

The ETA in Democratic Spain

1. Total amnesty for all political prisoners.

2. Legalization of all political parties, including those that advocate the creation of a separate Basque state.

3. The expulsion of the Guardia Civil and all Spanish police officers from the Autonomous Basque Region.

4. The adoption of measures to improve the working and living conditions of the working classes.

5. The passage of an autonomy statute that would recognize the national sovereignty of Euskadi, recognize Euskera as the principal language of the region, place law enforcement authorities and military units within the Basque region under the control of the Basque government, and give the Basque people the power to adopt whatever political, social, and economic structures they desired.

While these demands were a starting point toward the ETA (m)'s objective of negotiated independence, the proposal was unacceptable to the Spanish government. For one, some of the demands violated Spain's new constitution, which forbade any separatist movements. More important, the government did not want to be seen as rewarding terrorism. In response, the leadership of the ETA (m) took the position that they would force the government into accepting their demands by launching increasingly violent attacks.

A Return to Violence and Repression

Despite their stated willingness to negotiate a cease-fire, both ETA factions raised the level of violence within the Basque Country to unprecedented levels over the next few years. Between 1978 and 1980, ETA violence claimed 227 lives, wounded 213 victims, and included 19 kidnappings. The number of casualties in this two-year period was far greater than those due to the activities of the ETA for all the previous years combined. This wave of violence revolted the general Spanish population, which, having lost what little sympathy it may have had for the Basque cause, demanded a strong government reaction. More important, even a significant number of Basques began to view ETA actions as being too extreme.

A failed military coup in February 1981, inspired in part by ultra-right-wing anger with ETA violence and the prospects of a breakup of the Spanish state, sent political shock waves throughout Spain. In reaction, the government beefed up its antiterrorism laws and created a number of paramilitary groups that were sent to arrest or kill ETA activists. The most controversial of these groups, the Grupos Antiterroristas de Liberacion (GAL, an antiterrorist paramilitary group), was secretly supported by the government, which long denied any involvement with the group. The GAL assassinated dozens of Basques, many of whom had nothing to do with the ETA, in both Spain and France.

The coup attempt had a dramatic effect on the ETA (p-m). Its leaders recognized that they would be defenseless if the Spanish military overthrew the democratically elected government and that

A masked operative stands guard at an ETA press conference in 1982. The ETA generally invites only those members of the media that it considers to be sympathetic to its cause, knowing that Spain's mainstream media will eventually pick up on important ETA statements first reported by the select journalists. In addition to their appearances at such press conferences, active and high-ranking ETA members are usually masked when they attend the funerals of their fallen comrades.

the Basque cause would fare far worse under another right-wing dictatorship. They concluded that continuing to attack the current Spanish state would be too dangerous for the Basque people, for it would only spark more repression and the total loss of popular

A hooded police officer arrests an ETA political operative for his association with the separatist group. In the late 1970s, the ETA created a legitimate political party in an attempt to gain a voice in Spain's political system and explore the possibility of negotiations and a peaceful resolution of the conflict with the Spanish government.

A Weakening Movement

A number of developments throughout the late 1980s and the 1990s have weakened the ETA. These include:

- The implementation of more effective antiterrorism measures by the Spanish government.
- The sentencing of the entire twenty-three-member leadership of the ETA's political wing, Herri Batasuna, to seven years each in jail for collaborating with the armed group.
- The passage of bills to outlaw any political party that supports the ETA or secession from Spain.
- The joint condemnation of the ETA and Herri Batasuna by all political parties in the Basque region.
- A decline in public support for the ETA and its activities among the Basque population.
- French cooperation with the Spanish government in denying ETA members refugee status and deporting them back to Spain.

support. As a result, they intensified their negotiations with the Spanish government, declared a unilateral (one-sided) cease-fire, and, in 1982, disbanded in exchange for amnesty, the release of imprisoned ETA members, and the return to Spain of dozens of Basque exiles.

Although the ETA (m) was also concerned about the potential horrors of a successful military coup, its leaders remained committed to the armed struggle for Basque independence. Publicly, they ridiculed the actions of the ETA (p-m) and declared that they were against negotiations with the Spanish government.

Emergency officials investigate the crime scene of an ETA car bombing that killed a Spanish military officer and injured several passersby. Car bombing is the ETA's preferred method of attack. Terrorist experts believe that the ETA has perfected a way of setting off explosives using cell phones as remote control detonators.

Nevertheless, the ETA (m) and the government began engaging in a series of secret negotiations that would go on for years.

To this day, every attempt at a negotiated peace has resulted in failure, continued violence, and intensified counter-terrorism measures.

Spain Gains an Ally

By 1984, the Spanish government had gained another powerful tool in its fight against ETA terrorism: the cooperation of the French government. For years, France had allowed Spanish Basque refugees and ETA members to stay in France as long as they did not stir up trouble in the French Basque provinces. But with the death of General Franco and Spain's gradual transition to democracy, French policy began to change.

In 1979, France stopped granting political refugee status for newly arrived Basques. In 1984, that nation began carrying out active raids in search of ETA members and deporting them to countries in Africa and Latin America, such as Algeria, Togo, Gabon, Cuba, Ecuador, and the Dominican Republic. Today, France also formally extradites eterras to Spain to face trial.

A Brief Cease-Fire, a Shattered Peace

In September 1998, the ETA declared what it called a "unilateral and indefinite" cease-fire to help promote talks with the government. Although the Spanish government had always demanded such a cease-fire as a necessary precondition to negotiations, it quickly dismissed the ETA's cease-fire announcement as a stalling tactic that would allow the ETA to reorganize. The cease-fire ended fifteen months later in December 1999 after the government refused to discuss the ETA's demand for Basque self-determination.

During the cease-fire, there were no major terrorist attacks. Since the cease-fire was withdrawn, the ETA has killed several dozen people.

The ETA's Methods

It seems remarkable that the ETA has been able to keep its movement alive, given the many obstacles to its survival. The Spanish and French governments have been energetic in their efforts to destroy the group. Internal conflicts, splits, and desertions have plagued the organization throughout its history. Other Basque political groups and residents of the Basque region have increasingly condemned its activities.

Yet it is the passionate commitment to political and cultural autonomy on the part of a significant portion of the Basque population that allows the ETA to struggle on, despite the powerful forces arrayed against it. The group's organization and methods are designed to capitalize on this fierce and patient dedication to Basque nationalism.

Organizational Structure and Hierarchy

Because the ETA is a secret and outlawed group, the exact size of its membership is unknown and tracking changes to its organizational structure is difficult to do. However, terrorism experts estimate that, except in its early years when there were only a few dozen members, the ETA has included between 300 and 2,000 members, with hundreds of additional active supporters.

The ETA has a simple three-tiered, pyramid-like organizational structure. At the top of the pyramid is an executive committee in

In many instances, ETA operatives and Spanish police officers appear to be mirror images of each other. Eterras often wear hoods in public to avoid being identified by the authorities. Similarly, police officers are often hooded when they go on raids (as seen in this photo) to minimize the chances of being singled out by the ETA for revenge attacks. Government antiterrorist forces have also been accused by human rights groups of engaging in terrorist-like activities, including assassination and torture.

France, composed of about ten people. Each executive is responsible for one of the group's key functions, such as recruiting, intelligence (fact-finding and spying), weapons, finance, and publicity. The executive committee coordinates most ETA activities.

Below the executive committee is a loosely organized operational committee that oversees ETA activities in Spain. This committee has four to six members, with at least one member in each of the Spanish Basque provinces. Operational committee members are usually liberados, who are ETA members known to the police and who have given up conventional life to work full-time for the organization.

At the base of the organizational pyramid are commandos, or cells, that consist of three to five members. Each cell operates in a small area, usually in the town where they live or in a neighboring community. The commandos are often self-sufficient, work in secrecy, and are almost entirely cut off from the rest of the organization. At most, they will know the names of one or two other members who pass along messages from the ETA's leaders. This isolation from the larger group prevents cell members from revealing the organization's secrets, plans, or names of individual members if arrested and interrogated by police.

Finally, there are hundreds—maybe even thousands—of ordinary Basques who, though not ETA members, support the organization by providing food and shelter for eterras on the run and by passing messages between liberados and commandos.

Types of ETA Membership

There are three types of ETA members: the liberados, the legales, and the apoyos. The liberados, also known as ilegales or fichados, receive a modest salary from the ETA, freeing them from the need to earn a living. Because they already have a police record—hence the nicknames fichado (ficha being a card on file in the local police records) and ilegale (illegal)—they are the ones who are most likely to be called upon to execute the ETA's most dangerous armed actions, such as bank robberies, kidnappings, and bombings.

Basque youths wearing masks light a small petrol bomb following a large pro-ETA demonstration through the streets of San Sebastian, Guipúzcoa. The ETA's goal of establishing a separate Basque nation continues to attract strong support among young Basques.

The legales ("legals") are so called because they are not known to the police and can continue to lead a conventional life. They constitute the ETA's communication network. There are three categories of legales. Enlaces ("links") act as couriers who transmit information too sensitive to convey by telephone, computer, or mail. Buzons ("mailboxes") serve as drop-off points for messages,

The Typical ETA Member

ETA members tend to come from Vizcaya and Guipúzcoa, the provinces in which Basque nationalism is strongest and in which a greater proportion of the population speaks Euskera. They are also drawn from more industrialized regions where worker dissatisfaction runs high. ETA members tend to be Euskera-speaking men in their mid- to late twenties from middle- and working-class families. A small number of women have joined the ETA as well, though they are more likely to serve as apoyos. Except for the legales, most are employed. According to Robert Clark in the book *The Basque Insurgents*, 95 percent of ETA members are employed or students, about 50 percent have two Basque parents, and 40 percent have at least one Basque parent.

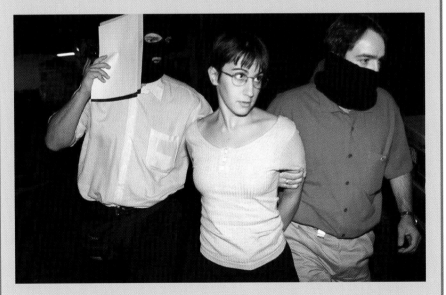

A young female eterra is arrested for her alleged involvement in a number of armed ETA attacks. A handful of women have gained notoriety within ETA ranks for their active roles in violent commando units.

weapons, and other items that pass through the ETA's network. Informativos gather intelligence about future targets of ETA operations. Traditionally, legales did not participate in armed action. Because they have a greater freedom of movement, however, in recent years they have increasingly been called upon to take on more dangerous assignments.

An apoyo (which in English means "support") is a member who supplies false identification papers, transportation, shelter, and other means of support to other ETA members who are carrying out an operation or are on the run. The term also refers to nonmember supporters who perform the same function.

Recruitment

Since its beginnings in 1959, the ETA has placed great emphasis on recruitment. Yet for security reasons, the making of an eterra is a slow and gradual process. According to Robert Clark in *The Basque Insurgents*, an older ETA member typically approaches a young prospective member at some event or club function and gauges the person's interest in joining the organization.

Once the youth agrees to join, the ETA member becomes his or her sponsor and guides the candidate through a number of simple tasks. At this point, the potential member is given very little information about the organization, so that the candidate will not be able to leak any secrets if he or she drops out. After a number of months of assessment, the recruiter determines whether the candidate is really serious about joining the struggle. If so, the candidate is invited to participate in a simple operation, such as acting as a courier of nonsensitive material.

This is the fiery scene of a car bombing that killed a supreme court magistrate and two other people in Madrid on October 30, 2000. Judges rank just below military personnel, police officers, and politicians on the ETA's list of targets.

Over time, the recruiter assigns the newcomer more challenging and dangerous tasks that pull the candidate further into the ETA's web of illegal activities. This makes it increasingly difficult for the youth to leave and gives the ETA great leverage over him or her. After about a year of these kinds of assignments, the ETA makes the young candidate a full member. Throughout the entire process, the recruiter remains the candidate's only contact. Thereafter, the new member will join a commando unit.

ETA Activities and Targets

Over the years, the ETA has killed over 800 victims, wounded more than 1,000, kidnapped 77 people, and committed a host of armed robberies, raids on weapons factories and depots, bombings, and a wide variety of sabotage. Most of the group's attacks take place in Basque Country, but a number of its activities have been conducted in France and in the Madrid and Catalonia regions of Spain.

The ETA's main targets are members of Spain's armed forces, who have accounted for 60 percent of ETA-related fatalities. Of the civilians who have died at the hands of the ETA, most of the targets have been politicians and police informers. However, about 9 percent of those killed and a majority of the wounded have been innocent bystanders or accidental victims who happened to have been in the wrong place at the wrong time, for instance when a bomb has gone off in a train station, park, airport, bar, or city street.

The typical ETA attack is the end result of a long and systematic process. The ETA executive committee in France, perhaps after receiving some intelligence from a commando, considers attacking a target. It passes its decision down to the member of the operational committee in Spain in whose district the attack would take place. The operational committee member selects a commando unit to carry out the operation and instructs its members to gather information on the target. The commando unit then reports its findings through a network of contacts back up the chain of command. The executive committee studies this intelligence and makes the decision on whether or not to attack. It also provides the necessary

Police officers assist a television cameraman as he exits a secret bunker that was used by the ETA to hide kidnap victims until it was discovered by the police in 2001. The Spanish media play an important role in the government's propaganda campaign against the ETA.

funding and, if necessary, munitions (weapons, ammunition, and explosives) to carry out the attack. This money and material is passed down through the network of contacts. The members of the commando then travel to the location, carry out the attack, and return to their home base, aided in their escape by the network of support members.

Funding and Arms

The ETA finances its operations in a number of ways. In addition to receiving donations from supporters, ETA funding comes from armed robberies, kidnapping ransoms, and the collection of what they call "Basque revolutionary taxes," which is actually extortion. Industrialists and other wealthy Basques are often threatened with attacks on their lives, property, or business interests if they do not pay the ETA this "protection money." Collecting weapons and ammunition has never been a problem for the ETA. What it cannot buy on the international arms market, it steals from weapons arsenals in Spain, France, and other countries.

The Future of the ETA

The stubborn survival of the ETA leads many observers to believe that the group's insurgency will continue for years to come. While support for the ETA has waned over the years, the quest for greater autonomy in the Basque region continues to thrive. Given that the Spanish government's police and paramilitary tactics have failed to destroy the ETA, it appears that a military solution is not likely. Yet if ETA history is any guide, even in the unlikely event that a negotiated settlement is agreed upon, the most militant of Basque nationalists will reject that peace agreement as a sellout of Basque independence, and the violence will continue to rage.

The United States's new international war on terrorism—launched in the wake of the terrorist attacks of September 11, 2001—may pose a threat to the ETA's continued operation. In February 2002, President George W. Bush sought to impose strict

Key Events in ETA History

1936 Spanish Civil War begins

1937 General Franco occupies Basque Country and orders the bombing of Guernica

1959 The ETA is founded

1961 The ETA attempts to derail a train of Franco supporters. The first wave of arrests and deportation of ETA leaders take place

1962 The ETA's Executive Committee is established by exiled leaders in France

1968 The ETA carries out its first planned execution

1970 The infamous trial of the Burgos 16 takes place

1973 The ETA assassinates Prime Minister Luis Carrero Blanco

1974 The ETA splits into two groups, the ETA (p-m) and the ETA (m)

1975 General Franco dies

1978 The ETA (m) creates the political party Herri Batasuna

1979 The Autonomous Basque Community of Euskadi is created

1982 The ETA (p-m) disbands

1987 The Spanish government holds its first direct talks with the ETA

1997 Twenty-three leaders of Herri Batasuna are jailed for their association with the ETA

1998 The ETA declares a unilateral cease-fire

1999 The ETA ends its cease-fire

2001 The United States freezes the U.S. assets of twenty-one suspected ETA members as part of a new antiterrorism program in response to the attacks upon the World Trade Center and the Pentagon on September 11, 2001

financial penalties on the ETA by blocking the assets of twenty-one people suspected of having links to the group. In so doing, the Bush administration ordered American banks to seize any money or property belonging to those individuals and ordered the United States treasury to impose sanctions on foreign banks or nations that provide banking services to the people on its target list. The move appeared to be a reward to the Spanish government for supporting Bush's war on terrorism. Nevertheless, it seems unlikely that the ETA will be a sustained target of the United States's antiterrorist policy, since it has never attacked American targets and is not likely to begin doing so.

If the United States's attention to the ETA does indeed waver, then the Spanish and Basque people will be stuck with a situation in which the ETA is no closer to achieving an independent Basque homeland, and the Spanish government has yet to solve its Basque problem.

Conclusion

A Harris Poll conducted online between January 24 and 30, 2002, and released on February 6, 2002, revealed that most Americans (58 percent) think that using bombs and guns against troublesome governments can sometimes be justified. Fifty-seven percent of the respondents believed that people fighting to overthrow dictatorial, military, or undemocratic governments are freedom fighters, compared to 11 percent who considered them terrorists. On the question directly related to the ETA, the American public was evenly split. Opposition to U.S. support for the Spanish government's efforts against the ETA ran at 51 percent, while 49 percent favored the U.S. stance.

Terrorists or Freedom Fighters?

So is the ETA a terrorist organization or a group of freedom fighters? If one accepts the FBI definition of terrorism as "the unlawful use of force or violence against persons or property to intimidate or coerce a government, the civilian population or any segment thereof, in furtherance of political or social objectives," then the answer has to be that they are terrorists. The ETA's goal of independence for the Basque Country is illegal in Spain. Its acts of murder, kidnapping, extortion, and bombings have created a sense of terror both in government and military circles, and among the general population (including among fellow Basques).

Even for many traditional Basque nationalists, scenes like this wreckage from an ETA bombing have become too difficult to bear. The ETA, however, views the continued bombings as a necessary means to an end—the acknowledgment of the right of all Basques to live in a free and independent state of their own.

The question is more complicated than it seems, however. Today, the American War of Independence and the fight against apartheid in South Africa are regarded as noble struggles for freedom and equality. Yet if one were to rigidly apply the FBI's definition to the actions of these resistance movements, we would have to label them as terrorism. At the time of their occurrences,

Residents in the Spanish capital of Madrid express their disapproval of the ETA during a demonstration in February 2000. Rallies such as this one draw large support throughout Spain, even in Basque Country.

each of these struggles involved what were then considered to be illegal acts of violence designed to achieve a political end.

The history of the ETA is divided into two main eras: the period under General Franco's dictatorship and the years since his death when Spain transformed itself into a democracy. When the repressive Franco was in power, the ETA received the collective sympathy and support of many in the international community. This goodwill granted them the status of freedom fighters, even though they were treated as terrorists at home. And even though the mainstream Spanish population is currently revolted by the ETA's activities, it joyfully welcomed the end of Francoism, which was hastened, in part, by the ETA's assassination of Prime Minister Luis Carrero Blanco—a fact recognized and appreciated by many ordinary Spaniards at the time.

Today, however, with similar actions by the ETA being directed against a democratically elected government, popular opinion—both at home and abroad—is turning against the Basque militants. The ETA's tactics and aims have not changed, but their targets have. Most people react with revulsion to attacks on officials who represent democracy, not dictatorial repression (though there is no guarantee that a democratically elected government will not resort to repression).

Perhaps the more appropriate question to ask, then, is not "Are the Basques terrorists?" but "Is ETA terrorism justified?" Maybe the fairest answer can come from those people whom the ETA claims to represent. Judging from the Basque people's growing distaste for ETA violence, despite their continued desire for greater autonomy, the answer today seems to be an emphatic no. To a growing number of them, the dream of an independent Basque nation is not to be purchased with blood.

Glossary

action-repression-action spiral theory A strategy developed by ETA leaders in 1965 designed to spark a national rebellion by provoking the Spanish government to react to Basque attacks with increasingly intolerable violence and repression.

buzon An ETA member who acts as a drop-off point for messages, supplies, weapons, money, and other items that need to be transmitted or transported but are too risky to be sent by mail.

commando The basic operating unit of the ETA; a cell.

coup A forced, undemocratic government takeover by a strong military or political group.

enlace An ETA member who serves as a courier or link between commandos, and between commandos and the executive or operating committee.

Enlightenment An intellectual movement in Europe during the seventeenth and eighteenth centuries marked by an increased appreciation for human reason, science, religious tolerance, and democratic governments.

eterra An ETA member.

fichado An ETA member who is known to the police and has a police record; also known as an ilegale or liberado.

Glossary

GAL Grupos Antiterroristas de Liberacion, or Antiterrorist Liberation Group; a secret paramilitary organization created by the Spanish government in 1983. The group was blamed for killing twenty-seven suspected ETA members before it disappeared in 1987. In 1998, a former Spanish interior minister and his deputy were sentenced to ten years in prison for their involvement in this so-called dirty war.

informativo An ETA member whose duty it is to gather information and intelligence.

insurgency An armed struggle by citizens against their own government.

legale An ETA member who is not known to the police and leads a seemingly normal life.

liberado An ETA member who is known to the police and has a police record; also known as an ilegale or fichado.

Middle Ages Period of European history between the ancient and modern eras that ranged from the fifth century to the fifteenth century.

For More Information

Amnesty International USA
National Office
322 8th Avenue
New York, NY 10001
(212) 807-8400
Web site: http://www.amnesty-usa.org

The Basque Center
601 Grove Street
Boise, ID 83702
(208) 342-9983
Web site: http://www.basquecenter.com

The Basque Museum & Cultural Center
611 Grove Street
Boise, ID 83702
(208) 343-2671
Web site: http://www.basquemuseum.com

Center for Basque Studies
University of Nevada, Reno
Reno, NV 89557-0012
(775) 784-4854, ext. 254
Web site: http://basque.unr.edu

Federation of American Scientists (FAS)
Intelligence Resource Program
1717 K Street NW, Suite 209
Washington, DC 20036
(202) 454-4691
Web site: http://www.fas.org/irp/index.html

National Security Agency (NSA)
Public Affairs Office
9800 Savage Road
Fort George G. Meade, MD 20755-6779
(301) 688-6524
Web site: http://www.nsa.gov

Terrorist Group Profiles
Dudley Knox Library
Naval Post Graduate School
411 Dyer Road
Monterey, CA 93943
Web site: http://web.nps.navy.mil/~library/tgp/tgp2.htm

Web Sites

Due to the changing nature of Internet links, the Rosen
Publishing Group, Inc., has developed an online list of Web sites
related to the subject of this book. This site is updated regularly. Please use this link to access the list:

http://www.rosenlinks.com/iwmito/eta/

For Further Reading

Alexander, Yonah, Michael S. Sweetnam, and Herbert M. Levine. *ETA: Profile of a Terrorist Group.* Ardsley, NY: Transnational Publishers, 2001.

Grinsted, Katherine. *Spain.* Milwaukee, WI: Gareth Stevens, 1999.

Kurlansky, Mark. *The Basque History of the World.* New York: Penguin Books, 1999.

Laxalt, Robert. *The Land of My Fathers: A Son's Return to the Basque Country.* Reno, NV: University of Nevada Press, 1999.

Lior, Noa, and Tara Steele. *Spain: The Culture.* New York: Crabtree Publishing, 2001.

Lior, Noa. *Spain: The Land.* New York: Crabtree Publishing, 2001.

Lior, Noa. *Spain: The People.* New York: Crabtree Publishing, 2001.

Ross, Christopher J. *Spain: 1812–1896.* New York: Oxford University Press, 2000.

Bibliography

Clark, Robert P. *The Basque Insurgents: ETA, 1952–1980.* Madison, WI: The University of Wisconsin Press, 1984.

Clark, Robert P. *Negotiating with ETA: Obstacles to Peace in the Basque Country, 1975–1998.* Reno, NV: University of Nevada Press, 1990.

Douglas, William A. et al., eds. *Basque Politics and Nationalism on the Eve of the Millennium.* Reno, NV: University of Nevada Press, 1999.

Holmes, John Pynchon, and Tom Burke. *Terrorism: Today's Biggest Threat to Freedom.* New York: Pinnacle, 2001.

Kahn, Joseph. "Expanding Financial Assault on Terror, U.S. Penalizes Basque Group." *The New York Times,* February 27, 2002.

Kurlansky, Mark. *The Basque History of the World.* New York: Penguin Books, 1999.

Medrano, Juan Diez. *Divided Nations: Class, Politics, and Nationalism in the Basque Country and Catalonia.* Ithaca, NY: Cornell University Press, 1995.

Ross, Christopher J. *Spain: 1812–1896.* New York: Oxford University Press, 2000.

Woodworth, Paddy. *Dirty War, Clean Hands: ETA, the GAL, and Spanish Democracy.* Cork, Ireland: Cork University Press, 2001.

Zulaika, Joseba. *Basque Violence: Metaphor and Sacrament.* Reno, NV: University of Nevada Press, 2000.

Index

Index

About the Author

Wayne Anderson is a freelance writer and editor who lives in New York City. A former music editor for the *New York Carib News*, the largest Caribbean American newsweekly in the United States, he has written numerous entertainment feature articles in such magazines as *Elle*, *Emerge*, and the *Source*. He has also developed advertising campaigns for various reggae celebrities. A self-described postmodernist, he maintains an intense interest in the stories of "the others" in society, which explains his fascination with the story of the Basques. He is currently working on a collection of poems.

Photo Credits

Cover, pp. 1, 5, 8, 36, 38, 43, 44, 46, 53, 54 © AP/Wide World Photos; p. 7 © Nelson Sá; p. 11 © Hulton/Archive/Getty Images; pp. 13, 14, 20, 23, 25, 26, 29 © Corbis; pp. 17, 41, 48 © TimePix; p. 35 © The Image Works.

Acknowledgments

I would like to thank Luke Rodney, Richard Sutherland, Michael Sewell, Hugh Japhatt, Al Rhoden, and John Kemmerer for the encouragement, support, and exchange of ideas that they offered while I was writing this, my first book.

And to the indomitable spirit of the Basque people for keeping their culture alive against incredible odds.

Series Design and Layout

Nelson Sá